FIND A JOB THAT FITS YOUR LIFE

Land Your Dream Job With This Personalized
Guide

Dennis Guzik

Quail House Publishers

Book Cover by Dennis Guzik

Illustrations by Dennis Guzik

ISBN 979-8-9878783-0-9 Print Edition

First edition 2023

Contents

This book is a tribute to you. Thank you for being present and investing your time in it. With utmost sincerity, I dedicate my Job Fit Process to empowering you with clarity, guiding you towards the right direction, and helping you lead a fulfilling life.

Introduction

You are about to embark on an adventure of discovery and clarity. When you are finished, you will have discovered new things about yourself and clearly understand what job(s) will fit into the life you want.

PROMISE: By completing the exercises in this book, you will find a job/career path that fits your life!

Personalized: It is your exercise input that determines the outcome. There are no "cookie cutter" answers - you control the data in and the results - - a job that fits your life.

Pivotal: Yup, the job needs to fit the life, NOT the life needs to fit the job. That is a pivotal way of job hunting and career planning.

Proven: Of course, you want a proven method. You don't want to waste your time and effort on something important and then realize it does not deliver as promised. My mentees and clients have reached success in their careers faster and higher than they ever thought possible. They are more engaged at work since their job fits their lives. Very soon, that will be you!

Process: This book contains a process that will help to identify what you want and need and what job (s) would allow you to have what you want and need. Soon you will have an answer as to what job would fit your life. Then, we will analyze which jobs to apply for and how to compare them.

Supplies needed:

You will need something to write with to complete the different assessments.

Preface

Are you ready for a "No Fluff" zone? This is how I write and coach: logically, honestly, and directly. If you are interested in a career planning and job-hunting process crafted by a military planner, corporate vice president, and operations research analyst, then you are in the perfect place. This is a step-by-step guide through the stages of the Job Fit Process for professionals seeking a career path that will fit their life.

I have used the Job Fit Process within my own career, and I have refined it over the years to help my mentees and career coaching clients.

Because I have used this process, I have been able to:

- Successfully navigate my two prior careers (military and corporate) and family.

- Mentor others and further develop this process to help others navigate their career decisions into a successful career that fits the life they want.

- Do what I enjoy and be a career and leadership coach.

- Have an impact and help others to achieve their dreams.

I have developed the best method for planning and hunting for your next job. My method ensures that your life wants and needs are central to your career decisions. This is the best way to achieve satisfaction with your life and career. That is why I'm so passionate about sharing this book that will solve the problem of Finding a Job That Fits Your Life. Finally, you can experience doing what you love, growing professionally, and living the life you want.

This book is for anyone looking for a job that will fit their life but is unsure what that job is. The process has several stages where your unique input personalizes the process. That will make the outcome just for you.

With each step in my career, I honed the process. I also learned new techniques that I could apply to the process. I had many career decisions to make over the years. As do you! I wanted a way to make the best decisions possible for my life wants, career wants, and opportunity wants.

This process works!

Why isn't this approach to career counseling taught? A change needs to happen.

So many individuals are unhappy with their careers and unsure of what steps to take, primarily because they did not approach job hunting by putting their life wants and needs first and then combining them with the other parts of this process. Thankfully, with my family, friends, and clients' support, I have put the Job Fit Process into this book.

Throughout my professional life, mentoring has always been a priority. I was lucky to have amazing mentors, and I want to be there for others and mentor them. It is part of my DNA. Through mentoring and now as a career coach, I have witnessed the power of the Job Fit Process and having a job where life can be the priority, as it should be.

It is time for you to have a job that enables you to live the life you want! It is time for your success story!

Respectfully,

Dennis Guzik

Thank You
Bonus Resources!

Resources are located at:

DENNISGUZIK.COM/RESOURCES

Everything to make the
job hunt easier.

Chapter One

The Problem: The Job Trap

M any of us know the feeling - you have taken all the necessary steps to craft a successful career, but instead, you find yourself unsatisfied and stuck in an endless job hunt. This phenomenon is far more widespread than you might think; countless individuals struggle with this same problem every day, unable to find fulfillment in their work life. For far too many, what started as determination leads to a sense of unhappiness or stagnation - underperforming in their current roles and being unable to break out into something better. It's time we reevaluate how effective current job hunting and career planning processes are so that people can get meaningful jobs they enjoy rather than being left without any hope.

What Is a Job Trap?

Consider this. The graph below shows time spent in a typical work week. The biggest block of time we have is free/play time. However, when we are career planning and job hunting, we have not considered this big block of time in our plans. We have not been taught to do that! Why? It not only makes sense to consider this block of time in your planning, but it is crucial! If you fail to consider this big block of time, you will find yourself in a Job Trap!

Average Weekly Hours

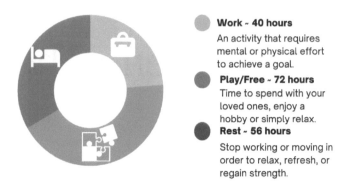

Work ~ 40 hours
An activity that requires mental or physical effort to achieve a goal.

Play/Free ~ 72 hours
Time to spend with your loved ones, enjoy a hobby or simply relax.

Rest ~ 56 hours
Stop working or moving in order to relax, refresh, or regain strength.

Could You Be in a Job Trap?

You can enter a Job Trap in many ways. The earliest is when you leave high school or choose a college major, a time at which you really have no clue as to what type of life you want to live. It continues when you take a job that sounds good, but you don't consider how it fits into your life.

Work-related stress, which can be caused by a
job that does not fit with one's personal life,
can lead to a range of negative health outcomes,
including anxiety, depression, cardiovascular disease,
and musculoskeletal disorders, according to a study by

the World Health Organization. [1]

Job Trap

Where recent graduates and/or professionals, at any stage in their career, feel:

- Trapped
- Stuck
- Unsure
- Drifting
- Underperforming because of following an incorrect job hunting or career planning process

THESE FEELING ARE OFTEN DUE TO TRYING TO FIT THEIR LIFE INTO THEIR JOBS!

We all know that finding a job we love is important, but knowing where to start or how to make the change is hard. Most people only look at their career options from their current perspective and don't consider their life wants and needs first. This can lead to settling for a job you're not happy with.

Job Trap

A "yes" answer means that you are in a Job Trap!

	Yes	No
Are you looking for a job that will fit your life but unsure what that job is?	☐	☐
Are you tired of being unhappy with your job but not knowing what would make you happier?	☐	☐
Do you feel stuck in life and are not sure what to do?	☐	☐
Are you searching for a smarter way of discovering the best job path for you?	☐	☐
Are you ready to approach your job hunt in a strategic and analytical way?	☐	☐

The Current Way of Determining a Career and Finding a Job is Ineffective, Rigid, and Costly

The current way of determining a career and getting a job is ineffective, rigid, and costly. Why do we let our jobs determine everything about our lives? It leaves people feeling stuck. Their job does not allow them to live the life that they want. Most career advice does not put our life wants and needs first. That is a critical flaw in the way career planning and job hunting are approached.

Ineffective: There are several reasons why it is ineffective to job hunt without considering your life wants and needs:

1. Lack of motivation: If you are not considering your life wants and needs, you may not be motivated to put in the effort required to find a job that you will enjoy. This can lead to a lack of enthusiasm in your job search, which can make it more difficult to find a job that you are passionate about.

2. Unfulfilling work: If you do not take your life wants and needs into consideration, you may end up in a job that does not fulfill you personally or professionally. This can lead to dissatisfaction and possibly even burnout.

3. Limited options: By not considering your life wants and needs, you may limit your job options to those that do not align with your values or interests. This can make the job search process more difficult and may result in you settling for a job that is not a good fit for you.

4. Poor job fit: If you do not consider your life wants and needs, you may end up in a job that does not align with your skills, experiences, or career goals. This can lead to a poor job fit and may result in you leaving the job in the near future.

Rigid: There are several reasons why the current way of job hunting, without considering your life wants and needs, can be rigid.

1. Traditional job search methods: Many traditional job search methods, such as applying for jobs through online job boards or sending resumes to companies, do not allow for much flexibility in terms of what you are looking for in

a job. These methods often require you to fit your skills and experience into a specific job opening rather than finding a job that aligns with your life wants and needs.

2. Limited job options: Without considering your life wants and needs, you may only consider job options that are readily available or advertised rather than exploring opportunities that align with your values and interests. This can limit your job options and make the job search process more rigid.

3. Stereotypes and biases: There may be certain stereotypes or biases in the job market that limit the types of jobs that individuals with certain backgrounds or experiences are considered for. Without considering your life wants and needs, you may limit yourself to job options that fit these stereotypes or biases rather than exploring opportunities that align with your strengths and goals.

4. Conventional career paths: Many individuals follow conventional career paths, such as climbing the corporate ladder or pursuing a specific industry, without considering their life wants and needs. This can lead to a rigid job search process and may result in individuals being stuck in jobs that do not align with their values and interests.

Costly: It is important to consider the costs that may be incurred when you are in a Job Trap. Some of these costs are obvious, that is true, but some may be hidden, such as in the list below:

1. Emotionally: Having a constant sense of dissatisfaction

2. Physically: Stress has an impact on health

3. Financially: Lower compensation due to poor performance

By taking a more strategic and holistic approach to our career, we can ensure that our work fits our overall life goals. This personalized approach considers things like our values, interests, and skill set to identify roles that will make us happy both in and out of the office. It might sound a little daunting initially, but trust me; it's worth it!

---

1. World Health Organization. (2019).
Mental health in the workplace.
https://www.who.int/mental_health/in_the_workplace/en/

Chapter Two

The Solution: The Job Fit Process

As someone who loves to help others plan and achieve their goals, it frustrates me to see the process of finding a new job or career path be unorganized and unsupported. It's often a significant source of stress in people's lives, yet the tools available to job seekers are often inadequate.

However, there is a better way. By taking the time to understand an individual's unique skill set, values, and goals, we can create a personalized strategic plan for finding the right job or career path. With this support, jobseekers can confidently approach their search, knowing they have a roadmap to success.

In this book, I explore this phenomenon and offer some insights into why it happens. By understanding the root causes of this dissatisfaction, we can learn to find true meaning and satisfaction in our work. With this knowledge, we can finally break free from the cycle of chasing after an ideal and instead create a truly fulfilling life. The bottom line is that the Job Fit Process will keep you out of a Job Trap.

Where you are today does not determine where you will be tomorrow. You make that determination.

How the Job Fit Process Developed

I have had two careers in my life before my current work as a career coach. The first was as a Marine Corps officer, and the second was in the national defense analysis/consulting corporate world.

During my time in the Marines, I gained in-depth knowledge of the military planning process and have adapted it to be the basis of the Job Fit Process.

During my time in the corporate world, I learned of a valuable tool for assessing business opportunities, and in this book, I have adapted it to the Job Fit Process.

I've successfully used these processes hundreds of times, both in my past careers and now in my current position as a career coach, and I can tell you that this works.

Straddling both careers was a master's degree in Operations Research. Operations Research is a field of mathematics that deals with using numbers to make better decisions. You'll see how I incorporate this towards the end of your journey.

Operations research can be used in a wide range of applications, such as optimizing supply chains, scheduling airline flights, and improving healthcare delivery.

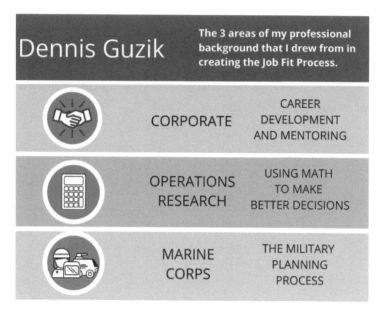

As you progress through this book, you will gain the knowledge and tools to assess your life and career and the impetus to make the changes you need to land the job that fits your life's wants and needs. As a result, you will avoid the dreaded Job Trap.

This process leads you to a career and job that fits your life, not the other way around.

Is finding a "dream job" the answer?

NOPE!

In today's world, we are all chasing the same goal: to find our dream job. We are told that by finding that perfect role, everything will fall into place, and we will be happy and fulfilled. But what happens when we land that dream job? Unfortunately, the reality falls far short of expectations.

Is finding a job that fits your life, as you want it now, the answer?

YES!

It is understandable that things may change. What do you do then? You do the Job Fit Process again! It works for finding your first job, changing jobs, and changing careers.

If you think achieving this change is a pipe dream, it isn't. I am about to show you how you can do this.

Chapter Three

Overview of the Job Fit Process

As we look at the Job Fit Process, let's keep the *goal of the process* in mind.

The goal of the Job Fit Process is a job that:

    1. **fits your wants and needs**

    2. **you are good at**

    3. **there is a market for**

This goal is what I call the "Sweet Spot". That is the center of the Venn diagram where all three parts of the Job Fit Process goal meet.

The Job Fit Process will quickly uncover these three vital pieces of information about YOU!

We can look at this with a Venn Diagram, shown on the next page. This book is not the first to use a Venn Diagram (I guess that would be Venn) for a career decision.

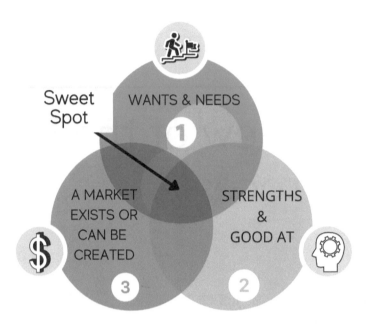

YOU HAVE TO HIT ALL THREE!

What Happens if Only Part of the Venn Diagram Goals Are Met?

If you only get (1) and (2), then what you have is a hobby or side hack, but not a job or career, because there isn't a demand for what you like and are good at doing. No one will pay you to do what you want to do. Can you create demand? Possibly. But if you choose this route, do so with open eyes that you have a real uphill battle ahead of you!

If you only get (1) and (3), you have frustration. Peers get promoted over you, and you don't have a good reputation at work, from both your co-workers and your boss, because you are just not good at your job. Not a good way to live.

If you only get (2) and (3), then work is good, but the rest of your life needs to be aligned. You have a constant conflict between your working life and your personal life. You wonder why you got a great job but still feel unsatisfied.

> Job seekers who have a strategic job searching process
> in place are three times more likely to find their desired
>
> job than those without one. [1]

Overview of The Job Fit Process

Now that we know where we want to go, let's look at the process we will use to get there. It starts with the Military Planning Process!

The Military Planning Process is the foundation of the Job Fit Process. The military planning process is a complex and vital part of creating successful operations around the world.

A tenet of Military Planning is that there are three levels of planning: *Strategic > Operational > Tactical.* The highest level is the strategic level, followed by the operational, then the tactical level.

Strategic Plans: Within the military planning process, we develop a Strategic Plan to support achieving our national objectives.

Operational Plans: we develop Operational Plans that specifically support achieving the Strategic Plan objectives.

Tactical Plans: we develop Tactical Plans that specifically support achieving the operational plan objectives.

So, the beauty of this approach is that it logically provides you with a path from lofty goals (strategy) to lower-level actions (tactics).

The military planning process also makes it clear that you have to get the strategy right first, then the supporting operational plan, then the tactical plan to be successful. No amount of tactical-level victories will ensure you achieve your highest-level goals unless you have this linkage and you get the strategy correct.

Within the Job Fit Process, we will use the military planning process tenets but apply them to support your search for a job that satisfies your life.

EXAMPLE: A simple look at how this can apply outside the military planning world will best show how this will work.

Let's say you want to open a store. You decide you want it to be a sports shoe store.

Strategic Level Goal- You own a successful sports shoe store.

Operational Level - You select sports shoes that support your sports shoe store (basketball, baseball, soccer, etc.).

Tactical Level - You decide on sizes to order that support your selection of sports shoes.

WRONG WAY:

If you get the strategy wrong, no amount of changing the sports shoe type or the sports shoe size will cause the sports shoe store's success.

If people come to a sports shoe store and see only dress shoes for sale, no matter how many types of dress shoes or how many sizes there are, the customers will not be satisfied, and you are likely to go out of business.

RIGHT WAY:

It's a logical progression. For example, if your strategic goal is solid, but the selection of items (operational) aren't sports shoes, you take these items off the shoes you are ordering.

Also, if after selling shoes (tactical), you decide you need more of one size; you order more of that size.

Applying the Tenets of Military Planning to Finding a Career and Job that Fits Your Life

STRATEGIC LEVEL:

- **Life Wants and Needs Assessment**–In your case, the strategic level is what you want from your life—what we call your Life Wants and Needs. Notice that it is not just what you want from a career or job, but the whole enchilada!

OPERATIONAL LEVEL:

- **Career Wants and Needs Assessment**–The operational level is what you want from a career. So we will call this the Career Wants and Needs. So, at this stage, we narrow down what we want from life to what we want from a career.

- **SWOT: A Strength, Weakness, Opportunity, and Threat Assessment**–Then a SWOT analysis is done to further focus on the career wants and needs. SWOT is a commonly used method for evaluating business opportunities. A business can evaluate an opportunity by assessing its strengths and weaknesses, as well as the potential benefit of an opportunity and the threats posed by competitors. But in your case, we will examine your strengths and weaknesses and the opportunities and threats for particular career areas.

TACTICAL LEVEL:

- **Venn Diagram and Quantitative Analysis**–The Tactical Level uses the Venn diagram and simple quantitative analysis to help you find the best jobs that fit your life. And, like the military planning process, your career must support what you want from your life, and your job supports what you want from your career. Do this, and you will have a job that fits and satisfies your life!

The military planning process is the foundation of the Job Fit Process!

Are You Ready to Find a Job that Fits Your Life?

Strategic Level: First, we start with the Strategic level. Remember, this is the most important step in the entire process! Because it is almost impossible to find a job that fits your life if you do not start with what you want and need from your life!

The strategic level is the first, and most important, element and the foundation of the Job Fit Process. This step is complete when you have your prioritized Life Wants and Needs List.

Operational Level: With our Life's Wants and Needs list complete, we proceed to the Operational Level within the Job Fit Process. Within this level, we will complete our Career Wants and Needs list and conduct our SWOT assessment.

When we exit this level, we will have our Career Wants and Needs List, our Strengths and Weaknesses Lists, and our assessment of the market opportunities and threats.

Tactical Level: Within the tactical level, we will use the information we developed in the two previous levels to build our Quantitative Decision Tool (QDT). The QDT will evaluate and compare jobs, including your current position, if applicable.

The entire process results in what we said was our goal—jobs within your "sweet spot," i.e., jobs that you want to do, are good at doing, and for which there is a market!

Simple, right? As I walk you through the process in the next section, you will see how simple executing this process is!

The Job Fit Process diagram shows you how all of this comes together.

The Job Fit Process
Find a Job That Fits Your Life!

1 Strategic Level

Exercise: Life Wants & Needs Assessment

2 Operational Level

Exercise: Career Wants & Needs Assessment
Exercise: SWOT Analysis
(Strengths/Weaknesses/Opportunities/Threats)
Exercise: Finding the Sweet Spot

3 Tactical Level

Job Hunting

Quantitative Decision Tool

---

1. "11 Tips for an Effective Job Searching Process." n.d. Indeed Career Guide.
   https://www.indeed.com/career-advice/finding-a-job/job-searching-process.

Chapter Four

Strategic Level: Deciding What You Want From Life

C ongratulations! You are about to begin a journey leading you to a job that meets your Life Wants and Needs.

I will guide you through this journey, explaining each step. I will task you with making self-assessments along the way, and from my experience guiding people like yourself through the process, you may even surprise yourself!

Let's get started.

We will begin this chapter with our critical first step, the Strategic Level Assessment.

This is the most important step in the entire process! The Strategic Level Assessment is the first essential step in ensuring that when we are done with this process, the job that you do every workday is one that meets your Life Wants and Needs and that you are not trying to fit your life into the demands of your job!

The goal of the strategic planning level is a list of what you want and need in your life, the big picture. Not just job-related but all facets of your life. What is important for you to have the life you want to have?

Please take the time to think this through. This step is the critical strategic step. If you get this wrong, no job will feel satisfactory to you. This is because although a job might be good, it does not lead to the life you want.

This list will be based on your values, ethos, goals, relationships, and current situation. I think you can overcomplicate this step. There are many books available to guide you through thinking about your life wants and needs, but we will take a much simpler and more direct approach (which we will do several times throughout the Job Fit Process.)

On to the first step!

Strategic Level Assessment: Life Wants and Needs

Step 1

The first step in the strategy part of the process is to think about all those aspects of your life that you value, find important, or bring you joy and a sense of satisfaction and fulfillment. Then, write them down. These can be as definite as I want to live in a particular city or as broad as I want to help homeless people.

The best way to do this is to take some quiet time in a place free from distractions and think about what is important to you. Consider what brings you joy or makes you feel fulfilled. Think about your family and other relationships. Think about your day, both at work and when not at work, and what satisfies you. This list can also include negatives, such as I won't live in a major city or take a job that requires frequent travel. Those are things that take away joy or fulfillment.

Examples of Life Wants & Needs

- The need for status and respect

- Time for family and other pursuits, vice getting on the corporate treadmill with the goal of greater financial rewards

- What your typical day, week, or year looks like

- Importance of things like time off, travel, and family time

- Whether you enjoy working more with people or technology,

- Working alone or in teams

- Working in the spotlight or behind the scenes

To show how the Job Fit process works, I will create a fictional person named Anita and use her to walk you through the entire Job Fit Process! Let me introduce you to Anita!

Example with Anita: Before Using the Job Fit Process

Anita went to a good college and graduated with good grades and a bachelor's degree in civil engineering.

Right before graduating, Anita spoke with her professors and the school's placement office, and they were all eager to help Anita get a good job as a civil engineer.

Anita had several job openings she qualified for, so she sent her resume to all of them, and three responded, asking her for an interview!

The interview for two of the three went well. However, Anita did not get a good vibe from the third interview, so she let them know she was not interested and waited on offers from the other two.

And she got them! Two good offers, both doing essentially the same thing, which was horizontal (e.g., roads) construction engineering, which was a good fit for her degree.

Since one had a better salary than the other, she accepted that offer!

The job involved moving to a new state since she went to college near home, but that sounded like fun, and the company offered to pay for the move.

She had a job even before graduating from college! Her professors and the school placement office guided her the whole way and were very enthusiastic that she got a good job (and the placement office stats improved also).

Three Years Later: Anita is Miserable

So now it's three years later, and she is miserable. She got her dream job (she thought), but why was she feeling so down? There were days when she did not even want to go to work. And her attitude was noticed. Her work was suffering as much as she was, and she could tell she was on a downward spiral.

Anita is in the Job Trap!

What should she do?

Luckily, while browsing through her local bookstore, she came across this book and tried the Job Fit Process.

So now, on to the rest of Anita's story.

Example with Anita: Life Wants & Needs

Anita followed the Job Fit Process, so her first task was to list the things she wants and needs out of life.

Anita took a trip to her local library, where she could find a place without distractions. She used her quiet time to develop her list of Life Wants and Needs. And this is her list!

Anita's Life Wants & Needs

- Be close to my family and friends. Be able to spend time with them
- A chance to contribute to something bigger than myself
- Eventually, have children and raise a family
- A job in a professional work environment
- Learn French (she is already fluent in Spanish and can speak a little French)
- Learn to play the piano well enough to play for others
- Live in an apartment that has other people similar in age to her
- The ability to meet new people, socially or at work
- A Master's Degree (not sure in what)
- A job with potential upward mobility

Anita was happy with her list, so she set it aside as she continued with her Job Fit Process.

Now it is your turn!

Exercise: Life Wants & Needs

Write down your Life Wants and Needs below (in no particular order), or use a separate sheet of paper.

Life Wants & Needs

☐ _____

☐ _____

☐ _____

☐ _____

☐ _____

☐ _____

☐ _____

☐ _____

Some of these may turn into a career field or actual job, others into hobbies, but we will get to that later!

Step 2

Now set the list aside for a day or two. Then, take some quiet time and come back to it. Ask yourself if you missed anything. Have you thought of something since making the list that you now need to add? After looking at the list, do you see something that is less important than you thought it was and should be taken off the list? You may want to reword some points.

It's tempting to skip this part and move on with your original list, but do not do that. It is worth a couple of days between lists. Your mind will continue to think about your Life Wants and Needs list over those days, and you may be surprised by how your list changes!

Example with Anita: Second Cut Life Wants and Needs

Anita set aside her list; then, two days later, she looked it over.

It still looked pretty good, but she thought that she wanted something nice when getting an apartment. So she would need a roommate to afford it. So she added this to her list.

Her list now looks like this:

Anita's Second Cut Life Wants & Needs

- Be close to my family and friends. Be able to spend time with them
- A chance to contribute to something bigger than myself
- Eventually, have children and raise a family
- A job in a professional work environment
- Learn French (she is already fluent in Spanish and can speak a little French)
- Learn to play the piano well enough to play for others
- Live in an apartment that has other people similar in age to her
- A roommate that she got along with well to help with the rent
- The ability to meet new people, socially or at work
- A Master's Degree (not sure in what)
- A job with potential upward mobility

Now it's your turn!

Exercise: Life Wants and Needs Second Cut

So, now it's your turn. Look over your list again, make any changes, and list them below.

Second Cut
Life Wants & Needs

☐ _____

☐ _____

☐ _____

☐ _____

☐ _____

☐ _____

☐ _____

☐ _____

Step 3

After you are comfortable with your Life Wants and Needs List, now comes an interesting part of the process. Show your list to someone who knows you AND has your best interests at heart.

Take a minute and think about what I just said. Then, let's break that down a little.

The person you showed your Life Wants and Needs list must know you. That typically means you have spent time together relatively recently across work and social situations. Someone, you knew well growing up but have not had much interaction with over the past couple of years may not understand in what ways you have changed, such as new interests. And, someone you just met, and get along well with, may not know you well enough to be a good judge.

The person must have your best interests at heart. That means they genuinely care about your well-being and success. The person you select may not be a good friend if that person seems always to want to bring you down to their level, vice help you achieve your goals.

Be brutally honest with yourself when considering who you are going to show this list. For example, a family member can be a good person to show your list to, but be careful. Sometimes they tend to think overly highly about some of your strengths!

What do they think about your list? Did they see something on it that you always find a reason not to do when given the opportunity to do it? Did they see something missing?

Consider their advice, but remember, this is your life and your list.

Example with Anita: Final Cut Life Wants and Needs

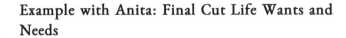

Anita decided her mother would be the perfect person to ask about her list. So she asked her mother if she would review her list and let her know what she thought.

Anita's mother looked it over and felt it reflected Anita well. But she did notice one thing had surprisingly made the list. That Anita had listed that she wanted to learn to play the piano. She had never heard that from Anita before. So was that really one of her Life Wants and Needs?

Anita thought about what her mom said and concluded that she was right. Maybe someday, learning to play the piano would be fun and important enough to be on her life Wants and Needs List, but right now, it's hard to call that something that she wanted out of life.

So, Anita's list now looked like this:

Anita's Final Cut Life Wants & Needs

- Be close to my family and friends. Be able to spend time with them
- A chance to contribute to something bigger than myself
- Eventually, have children and raise a family
- A job in a professional work environment
- Learn French (she is already fluent in Spanish and can speak a little French)
- Live in an apartment that has other people similar in age to her
- A roommate that she got along with well to help with the rent
- The ability to meet new people, socially or at work
- A Master's Degree (not sure in what)
- A job with potential upward mobility

Now it's your turn!

Exercise: Life Wants & Needs Final Cut

Show your list to someone who knows you well and has your best interests at heart. Think about what they tell you, then finalize your Life Wants and Needs list below.

Final Cut
Life Wants & Needs

- [ ] _____
- [ ] _____
- [ ] _____
- [ ] _____
- [ ] _____
- [ ] _____
- [ ] _____
- [ ] _____

Once you have your Life Wants and Needs List, let's see if we can prioritize the list, and then finally, let's see if you can put what is in it into some sort of hierarchical category.

Start by labeling each item on your Wants and Needs list as a Want or a Need. Be honest about this because if you list everything as a Need, you risk not being able to meet so many needs in any particular career field or job. There's an old saying that if everything is a priority, then nothing is a priority. The same thing applies here. If everything is an absolute need, then nothing is a need.

Look at your list and if you absolutely need an item in your life, then let's label that as a need. They are non-negotiable unless something else in your life changes.

Now, look at your wants. Let's break them down a little more. Some are really important but could be left out, at least for the time being, if we met all the needs aspects. Let's create a Really Want category and put those aspects into that category.

Then maybe some are things you want but do not necessarily need in your life. Your life would be better with them, but would not necessarily be empty without them, provided your needs and really wants are met. So create a category called Wants, and put those aspects into that category.

Example With Anita: Prioritized List

Anita's next task was to prioritize this her list. Yikes! She saw this book had some suggestions and put each Life Want and Need into one of the three categories we introduced earlier.

Anita's Prioritized List

Need (Non-negotiable)

- Be close to my family and friends. Be able to spend time with them
- A chance to contribute to something bigger than myself
- A job in a professional work environment

Really Want

- Be close to my family and friends. Be able to spend time with them
- A chance to contribute to something bigger than myself
- A job in a professional work environment

Want
(I understand that I can't have everything.)

- Learn French (she is already fluent in Spanish and can speak a little French)
- A roommate that she got along with well to help with the rent
- The ability to meet new people, socially or at work

After completing this list, it surprised her to find that it didn't take long, that it was easy, and that it made her realize why she is so unhappy with her current job. It fails to meet every Non-Negotiable Need!

She had to move away from family and friends to get the job; she does not feel that building roads contributes to something bigger than herself. Her work environment is mostly at construction sites, arguing with foremen and laborers about how to build the roads. As for upward mobility, her unhappiness led to poor work performance, so she can rule that out!

This knowledge alone is progress! It is not surprising that she has felt dissatisfied!

Now it's your turn!

Exercise: Life Wants and Needs Prioritized List

Prioritize your life Wants and Needs using the above categories, or make up your own and fill them in below!

Prioritized Life Wants & Needs

Need (Non-negotiable)

Really Want

Want

Step 6

Once you've done this, set this list aside. We will need it again! And, by the way, don't worry that this list is temporary. As life changes, this will inevitably change as well. The process will be here to help you when that happens!

So now, you have an idea of how you want your life to be, so let's move on to the operational planning level—planning for your career.

Chapter Five

Operational Level I: Deciding What You Want From Your Career

I n this chapter, we will build upon Chapter Four's strategic assessment that led you to your Life Wants and Needs List, and discuss determining your Career Wants and Needs. Like the military planning process, the operational level for our career is between the strategic — what I want from life, and the tactical — what job I want.

Unfortunately, too many people begin their career search without looking at what they want from life. Many start their career path by deciding on a college major, with little consideration of what they want out of life. And it's possible that a person of that age does not know what they want to do. The decision usually comes down to where they excel. Good at math? You should be an engineer! Good with children? Well, maybe teaching is for you.

Fortunately, you will not be in this situation if you have completed the Job Fit strategic assessment of what you want from your life.

Career fields can cover a wide range of ground. Take, for example, the health care career field, and consider who may be included as working in health care. Surgeons, doctors, nurses, technicians, pharmaceutical salespersons, hospital orderlies, and biomedical engineers all are considered to be working in health care. To varying degrees, they all share some common characteristics. For example, concern for other people's well-being.

The beauty of the Job Fit Process is that once we have determined what we want from our life, we can narrow that down and find a career field that meets our life needs while providing a satisfying profession.

When we finish this chapter you should have an idea of a career field(s) that will satisfy you.

What if the Solution Contains More Than One Career Field?

But what if you have more than one? That is not allowed! No, I'm just kidding. If you find that more than one career field would provide you with a satisfying life, then there are two ways of approaching that decision.

The first will be to see if there is a higher-level defined career field. For example, if you determine that chemistry and biology would be great career fields for you, then one approach would be to say that science is your career field.

Another approach is to have two (or more). Then you complete this process with one, your primary career field, see where you end up, then repeat the process with the other, an alternate career field.

What if I Already Have a Career Field?

But wait, what if you have already completed a degree and have a career field? Should you skip this section? No! If you are reading this book, you are probably not satisfied with your life. To ensure that your dissatisfaction isn't because of your career field, you should continue, regardless of your current situation and education.

You may find that things have changed since you got your degree, and aspects of that degree that you once liked you no longer like, or that once you got out into the real, working world, the real aspects of that career field were nothing like you expected them to be. It is better to find this out now rather than just changing jobs expecting something to improve when it won't because you are in the wrong career field.

So, no matter where you are in your professional life, I suggest you continue this process.

But if you are in the wrong career field, it is better to know this now rather than continue to suffer through life, wondering why you are unhappy. It can be a call to action!

Like within the military planning process, we have our strategic objective, categorized by what we find important in life. Make sure you have your list in front of you.

Career Wants and Needs

Step 1

Using your Life Wants and Needs List, the first step is to assess each item on this list and determine which can reasonably be expected to be included in or have an impact on, a career field (and ultimately your job). These then go on our Career Field Wants and Needs List.

For example, suppose you had sufficient compensation to travel overseas. In that case, then this important Life Wants and Needs item is something that will have an impact on your career decision. So it needs to be included on your Career Wants and Needs List. However, if you want to learn to play a musical instrument, this item would not go on your Career Wants and Needs List. Unless you want to be a musician!

The more things you put on your Career Wants and Needs List, the more restrictive your career options may become, so carefully consider what makes the list. For example, if something from your

Life Needs may or may not impact your career field, then I'd suggest you put it on the Career Field Wants and Needs list since this is very important to you. However, if something is from the Life Wants category, your lowest priority, may or may not have an impact on your career field, then I recommend not putting it on the Career Field Wants and Needs List. This is especially true if your Career Field Wants and Needs list is long.

But ultimately, it's your list, and you can put whatever you want on it!

Example with Anita: Career Wants and Needs

Anita will now move on to the next step of the Job Fit Process. She will now go to the operational level.

Her first task is to take her prioritized Life Wants and Needs list and consider each item on the list and decide if it's reasonable that satisfying that want or need should come from her career, or whether it is something outside of her professional life. If it is outside her professional life, it doesn't mean it's not important, it's just that she will need to fulfill that want on her own time, perhaps as a hobby!

After careful consideration, Anita came up with a list of what she wants from a career.

Note that she modified two items. First, she added "but with work provided tuition assistance" to her Master's Degree want. And she removed "socially" from her want of meeting new people but kept the "at work."

This is Anita's List, and she can do whatever she wants with it!

Anita's Career Wants & Needs

Need (Non-negotiable)

Be close to my family and friends and be able to spend time with them
A chance to contribute to something bigger than myself.
A job in a professional work environment.

Really Want

A Master's Degree (not sure in what, but with work provided tuition assistance.)
A job with potential upward mobility.

Want

The ability to meet new people at work.

Now it's your turn!

Exercise: Career Wants and Needs

So now you need to take your list and note which ones you think would have an impact on your career and generate your own career field needs list.

Examples of Career Wants & Needs

- A high interest for a particular type of work

- A strong dislike for a particular type of work

- A preference for corporate work, industry, academia, government/military, or maybe non-profits

- High interest in either the arts, science, engineering, technology, health care

- One that typically involves a lot of travel or one that usually does not

- One which involves a lot of long hours initially, with some expected payoff later, or one that typically does not

Career Wants & Needs

Need (Non-negotiable)

Really Want

Want

Step 2

Now find a career field(s) that meets your list. By meeting that List, you will also meet your life's needs and wants! There are some great resources and references that you can go to match your career wants/needs and specific careers. Three that I recommend are:

O*NET OnLine – https://www.onetonline.org/

"Welcome to O*NET OnLine, the tool you need for exploring different careers and analyzing job descriptions! We have detailed descriptions of various occupations from all around the world that students, researchers, job seekers, workforce development professionals, and HR specialists can use!"

Career One Stop – https://www.careeronestop.org/

I want to be a ...? Your source for career exploration, training & jobs Sponsored by the U.S. Department of Labor.

Bureau of Labor and Statistics: Occupational Outlook Handbook – https://www.bls.gov/ooh/

Occupation training and outlook information.

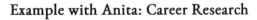

Example with Anita: Career Research

Anita starts with her current position as a civil engineer. Filtering her Career Field Wants and Needs list through the Department of Labor's Occupational Outlook Handbook, which she found online at the U.S. Bureau of Labor Statistics (bls.gov/ooh), she looks up civil engineer and from there, what are similar career fields.

She finds:

• Architects

• Civil Engineering Technologists and Technicians

• Construction managers

• Environmental engineers

• Landscape architectures

• Mechanical engineers

• Surveyors

• Urban and regional planning

Wow, how interesting. Besides her current career as a civil engineer, she did not know that there were so many other paths that she could take. Now a whole new world is open to her beyond what her professors and school placement office had recommended.

Some of these positions will require more education, which is fine as it can help her narrow her focus for graduate school. For example, with the appropriate certificates, she realizes she could also teach math.

After a little more research on what each of these career fields does and the environment in which they work, she eliminated some of the fields because of her realization that working on construction sites is not for her.

Anita's Career Opportunities List

• Civil engineer (i.e., different job)

• Architect

• Mechanical engineer

• Urban and regional planning

After careful consideration, she decides that the additional educational requirements needed to enter the field of architecture might be an educational "weakness" (Part of the SWOT Analysis, which you will learn in the next chapter.) Still, she will do a little more research before eliminating it.

Anita's Career Field List

• Civil engineer (i.e., different job)

• Architect

• Mechanical engineer

• Urban and regional planning

Now it's your turn!

Exercise: Career Research

Now it's your turn. Using the cited references and others you may find, see if you can come up with one or more career fields that will meet your wants and needs!

At this point, do not worry about whether there are jobs in this career field or even if you think you could get the education for that career field. That will all come later!

That was fun, wasn't it? What did you decide? Write it down here:

Career Fields

Primary Career Field

Alternative Career Fields

Now we will move on to the next step in our process, SWOT.

Chapter Six

Operational Level II: SWOT Analysis

Time for SWOT!

Job hunting can be a daunting task, but an essential component of success is to know what you bring to the table and what you're up against. One powerful tool that is used in business and that we will be using to assess your current situation and plan your next steps is a SWOT analysis. SWOT is an acronym for Strengths, Weaknesses, Opportunities, and Threats. It's an incredibly valuable tool as it looks at both the internal and external factors that could influence the outcomes within a business and in your job search. By understanding where you stand in relation to each of these elements, you'll be able to create a comprehensive and effective plan for getting the job you want.

How is SWOT Used?

Let's start with an example of using SWOT in the business sense to give you a feel for what SWOT is and how it is used. A common scenario for using SWOT is when a company has a chance to bid on a project. At that point, one of the first considerations is the result of a SWOT analysis.

SWOT ANALYSIS

STRENGTHS

What do you do well?
What are your good
qualities?
Where do people seek
your expertise?

WEAKNESSES

What areas do you need
to improve?
What resources do you
require?
What areas do you seek
others assistance?

OPPORTUNITIES

What career fields are
growing?
Where are possibilities
for advancement or
gaining skills?

THREATS

What career fields are
shrinking or are
crowded?
What factors are outside
of your control?

S –Strengths

First, after reviewing the opportunity, the company will assess its strengths specifically regarding that opportunity. Here, and throughout the SWOT assessment, brutal honesty is essential. It not only does no good but hurts the company to "rosy" up its assessment. Fooling yourself is not a good business practice, and expending resources bidding on a project you have little chance of winning (or successfully executing, should you win) is a poor decision.

W-Weaknesses

After assessing your strengths, you next assess your weaknesses. Again, brutal honesty is required. Having weaknesses in and of itself does not disqualify you from competing, as these weaknesses can be eliminated or mitigated in various ways, such as bringing on board teaming partners.

Strengths and weaknesses are internal assessments.

The O and T of SWOT are external assessments.

The next assessment is opportunities.

O-Opportunities

In the business world, this can include things like, should we bid and win this opportunity, then we will have a whole new customer base from which to expand.

T-Threats

Threats are primarily, though not completely, the competition. What do we know about the potential competition? There can be a tendency to make the competition 10 feet tall or one foot tall, so these biases must be avoided. Again, a brutally honest assessment is necessary. This is a theme you will continue when we take the SWOT approach to your career path assessment.

Let's look at how it will be used in helping your search for a career and a job that will meet your life's needs and wants. Once you have completed this chapter, you will know what you are good at (and what you are not good at) and where there is (and isn't) a market for your skills.

SWOT as It Applies to your Career

We will take the business approach to examine opportunities and apply them to your search for the ideal career and job. You'll notice quite a similarity with the Life's Wants and Needs Assessment.

First, let's take a look at strengths.

STRENGTHS

Step 1

First, let's think about your strengths. The first step in the strength assessment is to think about all aspects of your personal and professional life that you think are your strengths. Write them down. These can be as definite as I am good at inorganic high-temperature physics or as broad as I am a good team person.

The best way to do this is to take some quiet time and think about what you are good at doing or being. Consider past experiences, education, and evaluations. Do not worry about whether you like doing something you are good at. We will incorporate that aspect into the Job Fit Process later.

Example with Anita: List of Strengths

Anita is on to listing her strengths. After carefully considering her knowledge, education, experience, and what others have told her, she listed all her strengths.

Anita's Strengths: First Cut

Anita's Strengths: First Cut

- Civil engineering degree
- Good at math (she is an engineer, after all)
- Analytical – she loves to figure out things and is constantly doing puzzles in her spare time)
- Dancing – she's a great dancer!
- Cooking - A very good cook
- Dependable. If she says something will be done, it will be done.
- Frugal. She gets value from all her purchases!
- Honest
- Able to convey difficult information so people without technical degrees can understand what she means
- Speaks Spanish well
- Concerned - about the environment and the future of our planet
- Good with animals
- Gets along well with others

Now it's your turn!

Exercise: List of Strengths

Here are some examples you might include:

Examples of Strengths

- A very curious person
- A particular education, degree, or certification(s)
- A good public speaker
- A good runner
- Write well
- Physically fit
- Honest
- Studious
- Quick learner
- Good team player
- Initiative
- Tactful
- Unselfish
- Enthusiastic
- A good dancer or musician
- Quick to come up with innovative ideas

Did this list make you think of some to add to your list?

Write what your strengths are below (in no particular order) or on a separate sheet of paper.

Strengths

☐ _____

☐ _____

☐ _____

☐ _____

☐ _____

☐ _____

☐ _____

☐ _____

Step 2

Now set the list aside for a day. Come back to it the next day, and ask yourself if you missed anything. Did you think of something since making the list that you now need to add to the list? After looking at the list, do you see something that maybe isn't as great a strength as you thought it was, and maybe should it be off the list? Maybe you want to reword some points a little bit.

Example with Anita: Strengths Second Cut

 Like Anita's Life Wants and Needs, she set her strengths list aside and took a second stab at it. She thought about some recent purchases and now felt that she may not be as frugal as she thought (or wanted) to be. So, she took that off the List. Her new list now looked like this:

Anita's Strengths: Second Cut

Anita's Strengths: Second Cut

- Civil engineering degree
- Good at math (she is an engineer, after all)
- Analytical – she loves to figure out things and is constantly doing puzzles in her spare time)
- Dancing – she's a great dancer!
- Cooking - A very good cook
- Dependable. If she says something will be done, it will be done.
- Honest
- Able to convey difficult information so people without technical degrees can understand what she means
- Spanish speaking
- Concerned - about the environment and the future of our planet
- Good with animals
- Gets along well with others

Now, it's your turn!

Exercise: Strengths Second Cut

Take another look at your strengths list and update it below or on a separate piece of paper.

Strengths Second Cut

- [ ] _____
- [ ] _____
- [ ] _____
- [ ] _____
- [ ] _____
- [ ] _____
- [ ] _____
- [ ] _____

Step 3

After you are comfortable with the list, show it to someone who knows you AND has your best interests at heart. Recall my advice on who this person is from Chapter Four.

What do they think about your list? Did they see something on it that you consider a strength that the reviewer questions based on experience? Did you leave something off the list that the reviewer has always thought was a strength?

Listen to their advice, but remember, these are your strengths, and it's your list.

Example with Anita: Final List of Strengths

 Again, like her Life Wants List, Anita discussed her Strengths List with her mother, and, like moms tend to do, she thought her daughter had a couple more things to note!

These were:

• She is a fast learner of technical subjects (e.g., her engineering degree.)

• She is a fast learner of non-technical subjects (e.g., her fluent Spanish.)

• Looking pretty in anything she happens to wear.

While Anita did not disagree with her mother's additions, she thought the third did not belong on her list.

So now, Anita's Strengths Final Cut looked like this:

Anita's Strengths: Final Cut

- Civil engineering degree
- Good at math (she is an engineer, after all)
- Analytical – she loves to figure out things and is constantly doing puzzles in her spare time)
- Dancing – she's a great dancer!
- Cooking - A very good cook
- Dependable. If she says something will be done, it will be done.
- Honest
- Able to convey difficult information so people without technical degrees can understand what she means
- Spanish speaking
- Concerned - about the environment and the future of our planet
- Good with animals
- Gets along well with others
- She is a fast learner of both technical (e.g., her engineering degree) and non-technical (e.g., her fluent Spanish)

Wow, she thought, that was fun. But maybe not so much, the next step in noting her weaknesses. But, as the book says, she needed to be brutally honest here, so off she went.

Now it's your turn!

Exercise: Final List of Strengths

After showing your list to someone who knows you well and has your best interests at heart, make your final Strengths list and write it down below or on a separate piece of paper.

Strengths Final Cut

☐ _____

☐ _____

☐ _____

☐ _____

☐ _____

☐ _____

☐ _____

☐ _____

We will use this list to make sure that the career field and, ultimately, the job you choose is one at which you will excel. We will also discuss using this list as part of your resume in Chapter 8!

WEAKNESSES

The first step in the weakness assessment is to think about all those aspects of your life, personal and professional, where you think you are weak and need to improve. Write them down. These can be as definite as being weak at algebra or as broad as not being a very good team person.

Again, the best way to do this is to take some quiet time and think about what you are good at doing or being. Consider past experiences, education, and evaluations. Do not worry about whether you like doing something you could be better at. We will incorporate that as we progress.

Example with Anita: List of Weaknesses

After thinking it through, Anita came up with the following list of her weaknesses.

Anita's Weaknesses

- Writing – Hey, I'm an engineer!
- Public Speaking (see above)
- Direction finding – she gets turned around easily
- Understanding of biology and chemistry
- Tact – when frustrated she needs to choose her words better
- Cannot understand what some people see in modern art

Now it's your turn!

Exercise: List of Weaknesses

Write your weaknesses below (in no particular order) or on a separate sheet of paper.

Weaknesses

- ☐ _____
- ☐ _____
- ☐ _____
- ☐ _____
- ☐ _____
- ☐ _____
- ☐ _____
- ☐ _____

Here are examples of what others have had on their list:

• Poor financial management

• Lack of interest in working in a team

• Find writing to be difficult and not enjoyable

• Do not know how to swim

Do they make you want to add some to your list? If so, do it!

Notice that we only did one pass through this process. That's enough for now!

We will use this list to ensure that the career field and, ultimately, the job you choose is one that you can handle and be a good performer. This list can also be used to decide whether there are areas that you want to improve upon by making a concerted effort.

OPPORTUNITIES

So now, let's discuss opportunities. In the business world, we talk about opportunities in terms of expanding our market presence and generating revenue. But for our purposes, we will modify it to being about your career. What we are looking for is where there are careers and jobs where you can work that will provide you with the satisfactory life you want.

The opportunities we want to explore will be things that align with your career goals. This is a way of opening up the aperture on what you can do that aligns with what you want in life and what you are good at doing.

For example, within the healthcare career field, opportunities can include:

• Doctor

• Nurse

• Medical Technician

• Medical device sales

• EMT

We will use this list when we start exploring actual job opportunities, for example, in a keyword search on job boards.

For example, if you are interested in health care as a career field, nursing would be what we are calling an opportunity. I call it an opportunity because the compensation for nurses is good, and the demand for nurses is not expected to decline.

Below are some career areas that are expected to provide opportunities in the future. This list is derived from the growth rates for career areas from the DoL Handbook we discussed earlier.

Career areas that are expected to provide opportunities in the future:

• Genetic counselors

• Financial examiners

• Biological science teachers, postsecondary

• Operations research analysts

• Occupational therapists

• Management analysts

• Personal financial advisors

- Medical scientists, except epidemiologists
- Statisticians
- Physical therapists
- Software quality assurance analysts and testers
- Veterinarians
- Data scientists
- Medical and health services managers
- Biochemists and biophysicists
- Information security analysts
- Health specialties teachers, postsecondary
- Engineering teachers, postsecondary
- Chemical engineers
- Actuaries
- Nurse practitioners
- Software developers
- Physician assistants
- Computer and information research scientists
- Financial managers
- Computer and information systems managers
- Nurse anesthetists

This list will change over time, so keep an eye on it to make sure you are up to date when you think about your career and job choice(s).

Now it's your turn!

Exercise: Career Opportunities List

Using your Career Wants and Needs list and this website identify potential career opportunities that you find interesting.

O*NET OnLine

https://www.onetonline.org/

"Welcome to O*NET OnLine, the tool you need for exploring different careers and analyzing job descriptions! We have detailed descriptions of various occupations from all around the world that students, researchers, job seekers, workforce development professionals, and HR specialists can use!"

So, what do we do with these opportunities? First, we use them to inform our career decisions. They may guide you to fulfilling careers, as the threats we discuss below can warn you of possible job and career problems.

Another way to use this that could be useful is to look at opportunities (and threats) in a geographical way. In other words, some areas of the country may have more job opportunities than others, and this information may be helpful if you are open to relocating.

When we get to the job search part of, "Find a Job That Fits Your Life," these career opportunities also make great job search keywords.

Now we will move on to threats!

THREATS

The SWOT threat analysis usually focuses on the competition. However, in our use of SWOT for your career, we will take a little different approach, although it still does contain an element of competition (for specific jobs, vice business opportunities).

Threats can be for a particular job or across an industry. Think of opportunities as having potential benefits to your career, while threats are possible ways your career may struggle.

A career field that once held a lot of opportunity now may not be so opportune. This can occur for several reasons.

First, demand can go down. There once was a lot of opportunity for horse holders, but no matter how good you are, and how much you enjoy it, there is no demand for horse holders now, so deciding on this route can lead you to disappointment.

A career in which a robot or computer can also do the job, in which case there is a good chance it will, and then you may be out of a job.

The second reason for a career threat is that although the demand for a particular function is still high, the supply of people able to do that function is also high. This can happen when an area is "hot" and everyone going to college wants to study it. Think of computer graphics when advanced gaming systems were developing. The market gets saturated, and you could find yourself competing against many other people for a position. And, if you get hired for that position because of the number of other people who want that job, wages will tend to be suppressed.

Another threat that we want to be aware of is industrial threats. As before, there usually are multiple career functions within an industry, but if that industry itself is threatened you may find yourself out of a job.

A different type of threat is a career field that is highly susceptible to job-ending legislation, such as those that include fossil fuels

For example, the US manufacturing industry was once very strong. However, as globalization increased, and so did the ability to communicate and share data rapidly across large distances, more manufacturing jobs were sent overseas, where labor was cheaper. Other threats include cultural (think tobacco products), or legislative (think firearms manufacturing).

So, you could find yourself in what may be a high-demand job (say accounting) only to have to change jobs when the business that employed you goes out of business.

I am not saying that you don't do a job that faces a threat, but if you do, you need to go into it knowing that it may turn out to be a hobby, and not something you can make a living from. We will use this list to ensure that you do not go down a path that may not have the ending you want or that if you do go down that path, you do so fully informed.

Below are some career field threats that you should be aware of. This list will change over time, so make sure it's up to date if you use this process in the future.

• Postmasters and mail superintendents

• Power plant operators

• Computer programmers

• Electrical and electronics repairers, powerhouse, substation, and relay

• Power distributors and dispatchers

• Nuclear technicians

• Administrative law judges, adjudicators, and hearing officers

• Nuclear power reactor operators

• Nuclear engineers

• Chief executives

Now it's your turn!

Exercise: Threat Assessment

Use this website to find possible threats to your career.

O*NET OnLine

https://www.onetonline.org/

Threats

- [ ] _____
- [ ] _____
- [ ] _____
- [ ] _____
- [ ] _____
- [ ] _____
- [ ] _____
- [ ] _____

Next, we will be putting everything together to find your "Sweet Spot" of Jobs/Careers that would support your job fitting your life. That is the ultimate goal!

Chapter Seven

Operational Level III: Discovering the "Sweet Spot"

S o, you've accomplished a lot up to this point! Let's review the assessments you have completed so far.

Chapter 4:

- Life Wants & Needs–You honestly assessed what you want and need in life.

Chapter 5:

- Career Wants & Needs–Based on that assessment, you determined what you want from a career that will help fulfill your life's wants and needs.

Chapter 6:

- SWOT–You assessed your strengths and weaknesses, so you have an idea of what you are good at and where you would need to improve. You also looked at the market and have an idea of what careers and industries are strong (e.g., a market exists) that is likely to provide a secure source of employment and which are weak and may be at risk in the future.

So, now we need to put this together to see where we want to focus our job search.

To graphically show this, we will use a Venn diagram. If you recall from your early math classes, a Venn diagram is a means to show where "sets" of things overlap.

The diagram below represents this well for our Job Fit Process.

In the upper circle Number 1, you have what you want from a career. In the lower right circle Number 2, what you are good at doing, and in the lower left circle Number 3, where a market exists.

Where you want to focus your job search is that area in the middle, where all three circles intersect!

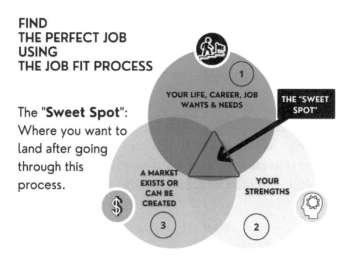

Why? Because it is here that you can find the job:

1. That fulfills your life wants and needs (professionally)

2. That you are good at

3. Where a career and jobs exist

This is critically important!

But what if you don't look for that three-circle intersection? Why not get a job where just two of the three intersect? That's good enough, right? No! That is precisely where most people get it wrong and fall into the Job Trap.

Let's Look at Those "Two out of Three" Situations

"Market Exists" and "Good at Doing" intersect:

You can find yourself like so many people that I have worked with, and who are the reason behind this book, in that you have a good-paying job that you are good at, but find your life unfulfilled. Something is missing. And that is because you did not align your career with your life. You are in a **Job Trap** and you need to change!

"Want From Your Career" and "Good at Doing" intersect:

Then you could find yourself unable to get a job, or at least one that pays the bills reliably. There is the risk of not being able to support yourself and your family. On the other hand, this endeavor could turn into a fun hobby. People who major in fields that they like and are good at but for which there are few job opportunities often find themselves in this position.

"Want From Your Career" and "Market Exists" intersect:

You could find yourself in a frustrating position of enjoying the career field and making a good living, but not progressing because you need to improve at it. You may find that your peers get promoted ahead of you. This situation is the most recoverable of all the two-circle intersections. You may not be good at it because you need additional education or training, which you can obtain. In this case, you need to enter into this kind of job with this understanding and then get that training before you become frustrated as you watch others advance in their careers and you remain stagnant. But there are other cases in which an attribute, such as a physical one, is necessary and you do not have that attribute. I, as a man in my sixties and over 250lbs, will probably not find good work performing in a ballet, no matter how much I'd enjoy it or whether or not a market exists for it.

When we finish this chapter, you will have the criteria you will use to evaluate specific opportunities. So, let's get going!

Step 1

The first step is to look at what you want from your career, derived from what you want and need from life, and compare that to what you are good at doing.

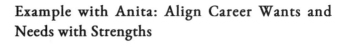

Example with Anita: Align Career Wants and Needs with Strengths

First, Anita must combine her list of what she likes to do with her strengths and make sure they align. Placing them side by side we have this:

What Anita Wants in a Career	Anita's Strengths
• Be close to my family and friends. • A chance to contribute to something bigger than myself • A job in a professional work environment • A Master's Degree (not sure in what, but with work tuition assistance) • A job with potential upward mobility • The ability to meet new people at work	• Civil engineering degree • Good at math (she is an engineer, after all) • Analytical – she loves to figure out things and is constantly doing puzzles in her spare time) • Dancing – she's a great dancer! • Cooking - A very good cook • Dependable. If she says something will be done, it will be done. • Honest • Able to convey difficult information so people without technical degrees can understand what she means • Spanish speaking • Concerned - about the environment and the future of our planet • Good with animals • Gets along well with others • She is a fast learner of both technical (e.g., her engineering degree) and non-technical (e.g., her fluent Spanish)

Note that we removed the prioritization from her list. We will use that later! What she is looking for here is where there is overlap. In Venn diagram terms, where the two circles, what she wants, and what she is good at overlap. After careful consideration, she feels that the overlap areas are **bolded** in the lists below:

What Anita Wants in a Career	Anita's Strengths
• Be close to my family and friends. • A chance to contribute to something bigger than myself. • A job in a professional work environment • A Master's Degree (not sure in what, but with work tuition assistance) • A job with potential upward mobility • The ability to meet new people at work.	• Civil engineering degree • Good at math (she is an engineer, after all) • Analytical – she loves to figure out things and is constantly doing puzzles in her spare time) • Dancing – she's a great dancer! • Cooking - A very good cook • Dependable. If she says something will be done, it will be done. • Honest • Able to convey difficult information so people without technical degrees can understand what she means • Spanish speaking • Concerned - about the environment and the future of our planet • Good with animals • Gets along well with others • She is a fast learner of both technical (e.g., her engineering degree) and non-technical (e.g., her fluent Spanish)

Next, she will need to look at where there is a market. Here we use her Opportunities and Threat List.

Now it's your turn!

Exercise: Align Your Career Wants and Needs with your Strengths

Your turn. Place both lists next to each other, like below.

YOUR CAREER
WANTS

YOUR
STRENGTHS

Now comes the fun part. Compare these two lists (and be honest about your comparison). Are there things on the list that you want, but are not good at? Are there things on your list that you are good at, but really do not want to do?

Note, that because there are things on your career list that you are not good at does not mean that this is never going to happen.

So now we have the start of our Venn diagram.

In the left, non-overlapping circle we have those things that you want from a career, but may not have the strengths to realistically achieve, at least not at this point. In the right, non-overlapping circle we have those things that you are good at but don't see as something you want in your career. Side note – these can make great hobbies!

Step 2

Now we need to complete our Career Venn Diagram.

We will compare the lists we just made, our Career Want list and Strengths List, with the Market Exists or Can Be Created.

To get the "Market List" we need to go back to our SWOT analysis. Recall that the Strengths and Weaknesses side of that quadrant were internal aspects of yourself and that the Opportunities and Threats side of that quadrant were external aspects of the job market.

We will use the Opportunities list we made and compare this to the Career Want list and Strengths list we just created.

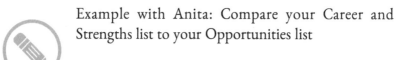 Example with Anita: Compare your Career and Strengths list to your Opportunities list

Anita looks across each career field and decides which of the Wants/Strength list above would also be needed in her career field.

Ultimately, she decides that the career field of an architect requires too much upfront education to meet her other needs. She wants upward mobility soon, not after years of education and an entry-level position. She also decides that continuing in the civil engineering field does not meet her career want of working in a professional environment (what a big decision – made in a rational way!)

Her career field inside the sweet spot now looks like this:

Anita's "Sweet Spot"

CAREER/JOB WANTS	STRENGTHS	MARKET EXISTS OR CAN BE CREATED
• Be close to my family and friends. • A chance to contribute to something • bigger than myself • A job in a professional work environment • A Master's Degree • A job with potential upward mobility • The ability to meet new people at work	• Engineering degree • Good at Math • Able to Convey Difficult Information • Concerned about the environment • Fast learner of both the technical and non-technical	• Mechanical engineer • Urban and regional planning

She now has defined her sweet spot, the criteria which, if met, will not only land her the job she wants but also the life that she wants.

Your turn!

Exercise: Compare your Career and Strengths List to your Opportunities List

Now compare these lists and see if there are aspects of one list that correspond with the other. This new list, which we will call our "Sweet Spot" list, is the part of the Career Venn diagram where the three circles overlap. You've done it!

Now it's your turn to make your "sweet spot" list!

This is where you want to focus your job search. You now have what you need to evaluate your professional life in terms that will lead to a satisfactory life! You've gone from what you want from your life, all the way to what you want from a specific job.

The beauty of this process is that when things change in your life, you can go back to it and work your way through it again and then see what you would now want from a job.

Think about significant life changes. That can be as major as a marriage, the birth of a child, the passing of a family member, or as minor as taking on a new hobby that may mean a move to another geographical location.

It can be used to see that now that things have changed, maybe I should change jobs as well. Maybe your current job still will meet your needs. Or, should it suggest a change is needed, the type of new job you should be looking for.

Chapter Eight

Tactical Level I: The Job Hunt Begins

W ow, look how far you have come! You started this process by developing your Life's Wants and Needs and have taken it all the way to defining what you want in a particular job.

Now you start the process of finding that job. There are whole books devoted to this process, but what they miss is what you have already completed, which is taking what you want in your life to what you want in a job. So, what I am going to do here is offer some advice on how to go about finding that job!

The Search

Searching for a job has never been easier. But that is part of the problem because while there are more opportunities for you to consider there is also more competition. More people can see what you see!

Based on my experience, here are some things to consider.

1. First, you must treat your search for a job as a job unto itself.

2. That means you dedicate time and effort to the job search.

3. If you sit back and wait for the perfect position to come to you, you will probably be sitting for a long time.

4. If you want or need a job, you need to get to work!

5. Set aside time daily to look for openings.

6. Draft a good resume and cover letter that you can tailor to specific opportunities. More on that later in this chapter.

7. Practice your interview skills.

Make yourself the ideal candidate while looking for that perfect job.

Networking

I am sure you have read that networking to get a job is the best way to land a job. And there is a lot of truth to that. For example, there are some future jobs that may be in the formulation phase (e.g., writing up the requisition and position requirements) that you can learn about by talking with people.

1. If you are not comfortable with networking and, in general, are an introvert who would rather not talk to strangers about a job, then you need to think about networking as a job that has to be done, like it or not.

2. If you are currently working, there may be parts of your job that you do not like, but you do them because it's your job (for now). It would be best if you treated networking this way as well.

3. Find opportunities, such as professional seminars or conferences.

4. Sign up and go, even if you would rather stay home. You need to develop an "I have to do this" mindset.

5. One of the best ways to get a job through your network is to get a referral. A referral is typically when someone at a company you want to work for refers you to that company's HR or hiring manager. That personal touch carries a lot of weight.

6. You will still need to apply for the job through their formal process because of HR concerns about fairness, but you will get a leg up on the competition.

7. I always considered referrals as a great source of talent. After all, someone working for me whom I trust (or they would not be working for me) has recommended a person for a job that carries a lot of weight.

Let's talk about job openings that you see on company websites or job boards.

They typically list a job title, a physical location, a description of the job and responsibilities, and then the job requirements (e.g., must have a BS in Computer Science). They may also list a salary range, as this is now a requirement in several states.

Here are some things for you to be aware of:

1. Companies put out job openings when they have, or anticipate having, a requirement for a specific type of person to do a particular kind of job or jobs.

2. You need to read each opening carefully to ensure you understand what they are looking for and whether they want you to do what you want to do (e.g., how well do they fit your Wants and Needs List; more on this in the next chapter).

3. Beware, however, that not all posted job openings are still active.

4. If there is a requirement, such as you must work from the office and you want to work from home, there is nothing to stop you from applying, but be realistic that you probably won't get that job.

5. Job openings typically have a closing date that is not provided on the job posting, so when you find a great job that seems to fit your Life's Wants and Needs, apply quickly.

6. Remember, searching for a job is a job, so even if you want to take a day off instead of getting your resume, cover letter, and

application squared away and submitted, realize that you may miss that opportunity.

7. Some companies will have job openings to see what talent is on the market. They are only hot to hire if the perfect candidate (which could be you) comes along. Also, when a company fills or cancels a job opening, it may take time to remove it from their website or job board.

8. Finally, it would be nice if a company responded to your application with a decision but realize this is going to happen only sometimes. You should follow up with a call to the hiring manager if you know that person or HR but realize even that may go cold. Put out your best effort, then move on to the next target!

The Resume

So, you've found a great job opening that meets your Wants and Needs. Because there are almost always things about the job relative to your Wants and Needs that you cannot discern from the opening, that is where the interview comes in. But to get the interview, you need to submit an application, a resume, and maybe a cover letter. So, let's get on with the resume.

First and foremost, the purpose of the resume is to get an interview.

Most people I have worked with need help understanding this. They think the purpose of the resume is to get a job. That is not true. Almost no one would hire someone they do not know on their resume alone. And understanding this is critical. Because people who think that the purpose of the resume is to get a job tend to put everything they have done or are good at in the resume, creating a long document that many hiring managers set aside to read when they have time but then never get to reading.

After 19 years in business, over half of the resumes I received were not worth reading more than half the first page. Very few left me eager to get the person in for an interview. My job here is to give you some tips that will get your resume read. So, here you go!

Before you even start to draft your resume:

1. Carefully examine the position requisition

2. Do you meet the requirements? Be brutally honest. You can apply for jobs where you meet most of them but do not expect a positive response.

3. They are requirements because the company thought about the minimum needs for the position.

4. How well do you do in meeting the "desired" applicant capabilities? Again, be brutally honest. You are in good shape if you meet most of them.

5. If you can show that you are working towards desired requirements, make sure this shows up on your resume.

6. If they provide what the job entails, does this sound like work you want to do?

7. Where is the work–at the company or remotely? Do you have a preference?

8. Investigate the company posting the position.

9. Is it a company you could see yourself working for?

10. Is it a large, small, or medium company, and does that matter to you?

Resume Tips

1. Keep it to one page, if possible. Two at the most.

2. Avoid the "wall of words" resume. Too many words, closely spaced, on a page.

3. Your name, phone number, and email address are all the contact information that you should put on your resume. No addresses.

4. No designs or pictures

5. Throughout the resume, use the same terms the job posting used as much as possible.

6. No fancy fonts that would be difficult for a reader (or scanner) to read

7. Don't bore the reader with information that is unrelated to the job.

8. Take the time to tailor each resume for the specific job you are applying for.

9. Sending in a generic resume makes the reader think you are either less interested in the position or are too lazy to put in the effort to tailor your resume.

10. Ensure that there are no spelling, grammar, or sentence structure mistakes. Have someone who writes well and knows the rules look it over. Spell and grammar check it.

11. The best resume speaks directly to the position and makes it clear that the person understands what I need and has the demonstrated ability to fulfill the needs of the job.

Resume Format Tips

1. Start with a short narrative that makes the reader want to continue.

2. Provide the most important aspect of your capabilities (use the strengths list you developed in the SWOT chapter here) that directly applies to the position you seek, and make the reader believe that you will solve the need they are hiring for.

3. Make them want to keep reading.

4. Provide a list of capabilities that directly (and only) apply to the position. Show them that you have the ability and desire to fill the need that they are hiring for.

5. Give a chronographic list of experiences that prove the capabilities you provided above.

6. No unexplained gaps. Use more lines for the more recent and relevant experiences, and less for older or less relevant experiences.

7. List relevant degrees and certificates. Note that this can be after the short narrative if the position has this as a focus (e.g., must have a Ph.D. in physics with an emphasis on particle physics).

8. If you are straight out of college, list any internships related to the job upfront.

9. I didn't put much stock into the references on the resume. Since the resume is about getting an interview, if I want references, I will ask for them during the interview.

Cover Letters

1. If you submit a resume for a job and don't know about cover letters, you are selling yourself short and reducing your chance of getting the job.

2. A cover letter is a way to introduce yourself in a narrative form that provides additional information to the resume and, if done correctly, will pique the reader's interest and make him or her want to read the resume.

3. Why should you submit it? Hiring managers and recruiters want to see it.

So why don't more people send cover letters?

1. They can be hard to write.

2. They take time, and it can be a struggle if you aren't a good writer. But what thing is worth something that doesn't take effort? Don't get lazy.

3. They expose your ability to communicate in writing. So, if you do this well, you are showing a skill. And hiring managers know this, which is why many want to see a cover letter.

What should it look like?

1. Your contact information

2. Addressed as precisely as possible.

3. No more than one page

4. No graphics (unless it strongly relates to the position), pictures, or weird fonts.

5. Make each cover letter specific to the job you want. It's easy to spot a generic cover letter, which often results in it not being read, along with the resume.

What should be in it?

1. Your contact information

2. Addressed as precisely as possible.

3. No more than one page

4. No graphics (unless it strongly relates to the position), pictures, or weird fonts.

5. Make each cover letter specific to the job you want. It's easy to spot a generic cover letter, which often results in it not being read, along with the resume.

Interviews

The dreaded interview, right? No! Approach it with a positive attitude! It's a great chance to sell yourself and learn about a particular company or job. Here are some tips that will help you get through the interview and make a great impression!

1. When you are contacted for an interview, ask for the names of those interviewing you if they are available. It's much easier to meet someone when you already know their name.

2. If it is going to be an in-person interview, you should do a route reconnaissance of the location on a day typical of the one you are interviewing on. Measure how long it took you to get there and where parking is if you are driving.

3. Never, ever, be late. Knowing how long it takes to get to an in-person interview is one part of this equation. The others are parking and how long it takes to get to the office and sign in. It's better to be a little (not a lot) early than even a little late.

4. If it's an online interview, ensure you and your computer are ready when they want to start the interview. Be careful about your background. Nothing that would imply anything except that you are a professional that the company should want to hire. One common mistake is to have a light behind you that makes your appearance either dark or haloed.

5. Dress appropriately. If it's a formal job environment, where people dress in suits, you should be as formal. You are being judged by your appearance. Don't wear anything old, frayed or soiled (I've seen all of these in interviewees). Make sure your shoes are clean as well, as this is often overlooked.

6. Do not wear anything that would take away from your being seen as a professional. Avoid a lot of jewelry, makeup, or perfume.

7. Greet the interviewers with a firm handshake and look them in the eye. Remember to smile. They are investing time in you, so make them feel that you are happy to be there.

8. Err on the side of formality. If Sally Smith is interviewing you, start by addressing her as Ms. Smith. If she wants you to call her Sally, she will say so.

9. If you are seated when the interviewers come into the room, stand up before you shake hands.

10. Have hard copies of your resume and cover letter available.

11. Know why you want this job and why you are qualified and rehearse this so it comes off naturally if asked, which you likely will.

12. Have the ability to take notes and take them.

13. Answer questions decisively, and don't ramble on. Respect their time.

14. Having researched the company, be prepared to show them that you know the company, its mission, products, and culture as much as someone outside the company can know those things.

15. Have valid questions for them. Remember, this is a two-way interview, and you need to decide whether you would accept it if offered a position. If there were aspects of the job that were not addressed in the position description but are on your Wants and Needs List, then you should be prepared to ask about them during the interview.

Cross the finish line!

1. Finally, at the end, thank them for their time, ask for a business card if they have not yet given you one, and when you might expect to hear from them.

2. Within 48 hours, send them a thank you email. If there is something that you want to emphasize, add that to your thank you note, and let them know that you are excited about the prospect of working for them.

There you did it! You found a couple of great jobs, applied with a tailored cover letter and resume, got interviews, and nailed them!

The job offers are rolling in!

So, how do you decide which ones to take? Read the next chapter!

Chapter Nine

Tactical Level II: Discover The Best Job Offer To Accept

So, you've worked your way through this great guidebook, and now you have a list of what you want in a job that will result in a satisfying life.

Now it's time to decide on that job!

What I will show you is a way to evaluate:

- Your prospective jobs in order to gain insights into which job to pursue. There is no sense in putting your energy toward a job you do not want or that will not ultimately lead to a satisfying life.

- The job offer you should accept that will lead you to a satisfying life.

This model will involve a little math. Very little, I promise you. Don't be afraid!

This process is straightforward, and I am going to walk you through this, step by step. If you can add and multiply, use a calculator, or work in a spreadsheet. You can do this!

On math:

> **"Do not worry about your difficulties in Mathematics. I can assure you mine are still greater."**

> **– Albert Einstein wrote in a letter to high school student Barbara Lee Wilson**

There are two ways you can do this, on paper or in a spreadsheet. I recommend a spreadsheet since it's a lot easier to make changes, and you won't have math errors (but you may have other errors if you are not careful.)

It is important to note that what we are creating is a model. A model is just a representation of reality. It's also important to note that this model will not tell you what to do or not to do. Only you should make that decision. This model will exist only to give you insights that you may not have been able to get just by looking at the raw information in front of you.

At the end of this chapter, you will have a model that you can use to evaluate your prospective jobs with insights into how well they match your needs and will result in a satisfying life.

An Introduction to Simple Quantitative Decision Tools (QDT)

Now, what do I mean by "quantitative decision tools"? The QDT may be new to you but do not be dismayed. It is easier than you think and truly separates the Job Fit Process from other career and job advice books.

The QDT uses numbers to help you gain insight into a decision to help you make that decision.

Does it mean that the numbers tell you what to do? Nope. They help you along.

We are all aware of qualitative decision-making. For example, if I say that the hamburger at one restaurant is good and another is very good, we are making a qualitative judgment about those two hamburgers. We do not have a definitive way of saying how much better the very good is than the good. But it's a start in our decision-making process on where to buy a hamburger.

We can take qualitative a little further. For example, you may have seen stoplight charts. These stoplight charts are a way of describing the attributes of a product. Typically, green is good, yellow fair, and red poor. A single product may have several attributes that can be ranked this way.

Now we can take this even further by assigning numbers to each attribute! You've probably done this already. Think about when someone asked you, say, on a scale of one to five, how much you like something. Or when a doctor asks you to assess your pain on a scale of one to ten. It's that simple. The doctor assigns a zero to no pain and a 10 to immense pain. For this assessment, you will do something similar; only you will be rating how important an aspect of your life, career, or job is to you.

Applying a QDT to Finding a Job that Fits Your Life

1. Once your Career Wants and Needs are prioritized, we use that information to build the QDT.

2. The QDT will then compare jobs against each other and your current job if you have one.

3. Ultimately, you will use this simple tool to get insights into how well any particular job will fit your Life Wants and Need

4. We will take all the factors in your "sweet spot" and for each potential job, or job offer, evaluate whether that job meets your factors.

If you have six "Sweet Spot" factors and are looking at two jobs, you could do something like this, where we put an x if that job meets your factor:

	Job 1	Job 2
Factor 1	x	
Factor 2	x	x
Factor 3	x	
Factor 4		x
Factor 5	x	
Factor 6	x	x
Total Score	5	3

So, as you can see, Job 1 appears to be better than Job 2. So, if you are deciding where to apply, then put more focus on applying to Job 1 over Job 2. Of course, you can still apply to Job 2, but not at the expense of applying to Job 1.

Pretty simple, and I would guess that you have done something similar for other decisions you have made.

Adding Your Wants and Needs List

But let's take that a little further. Let's say that not all factors are of equal importance. This is where we go back to our prioritized Wants and Needs List, where we put each factor into one of three categories: Need (non-negotiable), Really Want, and Want.

Our QDT might look like this:

	Prioritization	Job 1	Job 2
Factor 1	Need	x	
Factor 2	Need	x	x
Factor 3	Really Want	x	
Factor 4	Really Want		x
Factor 5	Want	x	
Factor 6	Want	x	x
Total Score		5	3

Now we have a little more insight into each job. Whereas the score does not change from our first model, it is clear that Job 2 does not meet one of the factors that we felt when we started this process was a Need. This is important because should you take Job 2, you would need to do it with the awareness that something you felt was essential in your life would not be there with Job 2.

Assigning a Level of Importance or Weight

We can take this even further by assigning a level of importance (or weight) to each category. So, for example, we can say that Need is a 3, a Really Want is a 2, and a Want is a 1.

Are these somewhat arbitrary?

Yes, so you can make up your own numbers. The only rule is that the Need has to be greater than the Really Want, and the Really Want has to be greater than the Want. How much greater is up to you.

Need > Really Want > Want (for the math geeks)

So, here is where we would be:

	Prioritization	Importance	Job 1	Job 2
Factor 1	Need	3	3	
Factor 2	Need	3	3	3
Factor 3	Really Want	2	2	
Factor 4	Really Want	2		2
Factor 5	Want	1	1	
Factor 6	Want	1	1	1
Total Score			10	6

Note that I replaced the x's with the importance score for each job. So now we can sum this up for our new job scores.

We learned that while the scores were pretty close when we first started, Job 1 seems to be a lot better now.

Now we will take it to the furthest we are going to go. Instead of just saying a Job meets a factor, we are going to assess how much it does so. This is important because, for example, you say that you want to live close to family, and one job is 20 minutes away, and another is 2 hours away, you may still feel each is close to family, but one is clearly closer.

Adding a Percentage

So, let's look at the QDT now that we added a percentage of how much a job meets a factor.

	Prioritization	Importance	Job 1 % Meets Factor	Job 1 Factor Score	Job 2 % Meets Factor	Job 2 Factor Score
Factor 1	Need	3	100%	3	0%	0
Factor 2	Need	3	100%	3	100%	3
Factor 3	Really Want	2	50%	1	0%	0
Factor 4	Really Want	2			100%	2
Factor 5	Want	1	50%	0.5	0%	
Factor 6	Want	1	100%	1	100%	1
Total Score				8.5		6

So, now you have a simple model that you can use to assess potential jobs and actual job offers.

As a side mention, there are two other uses for this model.

- You can use this to assess your current job if you have one. Just do the same thing, but instead of Job 1, use your current job, then assess it the same way. You may not be surprised to see how badly it scores. That is why you feel poorly about your job and want to move on. This shows that you are in a Job Trap!

- You can compare your current job score to any potential job score to see how much better a new job would be. We know the grass is always greener on the other side of the fence, but it might surprise you to see how much (or how little) a new job is compared to what you have.

- You can come up with your ultimate job score simply by assuming that job would meet 100% of every Want and Need. Just add the Importance column; in our example, that would be 12. So, you can see how close (or far away) a potential job is from what you want. This could make you consider continuing your job search instead of taking what is now available.

Example with Anita: Quantitative Data Analysis of Job Opportunities

Anita is now ready to move on to the tactical part of her path to find a job that fits her life!

Anita uses her networking skills, online job boards, and other sources of opportunities based on her career path as a mechanical engineer or urban and regional planning.

The market for those careers is pretty good, but she knew that already because of her Opportunities and Threats assessments.

She finds five potential jobs, three as a mechanical engineer and two as an urban and regional planner, that she thinks will be a good fit. Here they are:

- Mechanical Engineer at the Star Company

- Mechanical Engineer at the Ace Company

- Mechanical Engineer at the Delta Company

- Urban and Regional Planner at the Jones Company

- Urban and Regional Planner at the Smith Company

From her "Sweet Spot" analysis, she has the following factors to consider:

- A mechanical engineering job

- A regional and urban planning job

- A job close to my family and friends.

- A job that gives me a chance to contribute to something bigger

- A job in a professional work environment

- A job that will tuition support my goal of getting a Master's Degree

- A job with potential upward mobility

- The ability to meet new people at work

Now, she does further research on each of these companies and put her evaluation scores into the model to see which ones she should take the time to submit a cover letter and resume to and if she had a lot of job openings, that would be a good idea.

But for now, she decides to send a cover letter and resume to each and see if she can get an interview.

Anita tailored her resume and cover letter, adding relevant strengths from her strength list, and submitted it for each opportunity. She heard back from 4 of the 5 companies (she never heard back from Star Co, which any job seeker will tell you is not unusual), and they are all asking her to come in for an interview!

Her QDT looks like this:

	Me at Ace	Me at Delta	U&RP at Jones	U&RP at Smith
Close to family and friends				
Contribute				
Prof. work environ.				
Tuition Support				
Upword mobility				
Meet new people				
TOTAL SCORE				

From what she can determine from her research on each company she puts an X in each box if she believes that the company meets her Sweet Spot, so her **QDT now looks like this:**

	Me at Ace	Me at Delta	U&RP at Jones	U&RP at Smith
Close to family and friends	X		X	X
Contribute	X	X	X	X
Prof. work environ.	X	X	X	X
Tuition Support		X	X	X
Upword mobility	X	X	X	
Meet new people	X	X	X	X
TOTAL SCORE	5	5	6	5

There isn't a very good separation between the jobs! Her QDT needs to provide more information to make a good determination about which job is the best.

As she prepares for each interview, she knows interviews are two-way streets. Of course, the company is assessing if you are a good fit for them, but Anita knows that she also needs to evaluate if this is a place where she wants to work. A place that will align with her Life's Wants and Needs.

But she also knows that following the Job Fit Process, the key information she needs to get is the "sweet spot" information in her model.

She develops these questions:

1. Where is the job located? (A job close to my family and friends)

2. Will I be working on something in which I will be contributing to something good for society? (A job that gives me a chance to contribute to something bigger than myself)

3. Please tell me about the office environment that I will be working in. (A job in a professional work environment)

4. Do you have a tuition assistance benefit, and how much is it? (A job that will tuition support my goal of getting a Master's Degree)

5. What is my likely next step if I do well, and how is that evaluated? (A job with potential upward mobility)

6. Will I be working alone or in teams? Will I work on multiple projects or just one at a time (The ability to meet new people at work)

After all of the interviews were completed, she gathered the information she needed to make an informed decision.

She gets offers from three of the four companies (Smith declined to make her an offer).

She evaluates each of the companies that made her offers, using the scale of:

0 – The Company does not meet this job want

1 – The Company slightly meets the job want

2 – The Company meets the job want

3 – The Company exceeds the job want

Her matrix now looks like this:

	Me at Ace	Me at Delta	U&RP at Jones
Close to family and friends	3	1	3
Contribute	1	2	2
Prof. work environ.	2	2	2
Tuition Support	0	3	2
Upword mobility	1	3	2
Meet new people	2	3	3
TOTAL SCORE	9	14	14

Anita is starting to see some separation between the mechanical engineering job at ACE and the other two jobs, but there isn't any separation between those other two jobs (mechanical engineering at Delta and Urban and Regional Planner at Jones).

She realizes that taking the QDT to the next step is necessary!

Anita goes back to her prioritized list of wants and notes the following rankings of how important each want and need is:

- Close to family – Need

- Contribute -- Need

- Prof Environ -- Need

- Tuition Support – Really Want

- Upward Mobility – Really Want

- Meet new people – Want

She uses this information to come up with her weights.

This is her call, but to keep it simple for her first run-through, she decides to weigh the job attributes as such:

- Need – 3 points

- Really Want – 2 points

- Want – 1 point

She puts that into her model, so now her model looks like this:

	Weight	Me at Ace Eval.	Me at Ace Score	Me at Delta Eval.	Me at Delta Score	U&RP at Jones Eval.	U&RP at Jones Score
Close to family and friends	3	3	9	1	3	3	9
Contribute	3	1	3	2	6	2	6
Prof. work environ.	3	2	6	2	6	2	6
Tuition Support	2	0	0	3	6	2	4
Upword mobility	2	1	2	3	6	2	4
Meet new people	1	2	2	3	3	3	3
TOTAL SCORE			22		30		32

Let's take a closer look at these scores and their meaning. Remember, the model does not tell you what to do; it just provides insight into your decision-making, taking in a lot of information and simplifying it for your decision.

The total score for the mechanical engineering position at Ace Co. was 22, which was well below the other two options. For this to be a good choice, additional factors must be involved, such as the compensation they offered was really good. However, Anita knows that she needs to be very careful about that because when given the opportunity to rank compensation as a key life and career factor she chose not to. She may be making a similar mistake to her current situation if she accepts a job at Ace Co because of non-life/career goals and then finds herself unhappy.

The scores of both the mechanical engineering job at Delta Co. and the Urban and Regional Planning job at Jones Co are similar, enough so that Anita should take a closer look before choosing one over the other.

Upon doing so, what becomes evident is that the engineering position is not located close to family.

Recall that she said this was non-negotiable. Since this is the case, there is a solid reason to reject this job offer, even though it is close enough in score to the Urban and Regional Planning job to look at other factors, such as compensation.

Anita ultimately decides to take the Urban and Regional Planning position!

Flash forward another six months, and Anita is thrilled with her new job! She is excelling because she enjoys going to work, and it shows in the quality of her work.

The process worked, as it has for others many times.

Life will hand you changes, such as starting a family or changing marital status. However, when it does, the process is there for you to re-evaluate your situation so you don't find yourself dissatisfied with your job, even though it was exactly what you wanted at one point!

Now it's your turn!

Now you get to have the fun of creating your very own QDT!

Simply follow the example above using your factors (sweet spot, wants, and needs) and job opportunities. Then, walk through the process until you have the insights you need to make your decision.

Below are some tips and alternative scoring methods that you can use.

For measuring how well a job meets your criterion

For evaluation criteria, instead of just putting an X or 1 if it meets that criterion, you can try this:

<u>Evaluation   Meaning</u>

0   This job does not fulfill my particular job want at all.

1   This job will fulfill my particular job want a little bit.

2   This job fulfills my particular job want, but only partially. Or I am not sure.

3   This job will mostly fulfill my particular job want.

4   This job will completely fulfill my particular job want.

Seem reasonable? You are only trying to gain insight into your decision, so if this helps, use it!

For giving a weight to each of your Wants and Needs:

Let's explore another way of determining weights for each want and need.

Like the evaluation scoring, there are many ways of doing this, but here is a good one:

If a particular job want is vitally important to you, then give it a 1.

If a particular job want is of absolutely no value to you, then give it a 0 (zero).

You may ask, why is it on the list of job wants if I give it a zero? Good question! When you first built this model, you thought it was important, but later, you realized that might not be the case.

Instead of having to delete it and do the math, you give it a zero and move on.

So let's use this for our weights:

Weight   Reason

0   This job want or need is no longer important to me

0.25 (1/4)   This job want or need is between no longer important and kind of important to my satisfaction

0.5 (1/2)   This job want or need is kind of important to my satisfaction

0.75 (3/4)   This job want or need is between kind of important and vital to my satisfaction

1.0   This job want or need is vital to my satisfaction

You can also use any other number between zero and one, you are not limited to just these numbers, but they all must relate to the other numbers because the importance increases as the number does.

The table below is an example that you can use to build your own model.

Sweet Spot Factor	Weight	Job 1 Eval.	Job 1 Score	Job 2 Eval.	Job 2 Score
Example: Good Pay	w	a	w x a	b	w x b
Total Score			Total		Total

For Evaluating the Final Job Scores

After you have built your model and determined each job score, set it aside and look at it again later or the next day. Do you still feel the particular job scores are the same? How about the weights? The good thing about building this model in a spreadsheet is that you can quickly change those numbers and see what results you get.

There are two things that you should consider:

1. First is what is called dominance. That means that no matter how much we reasonably change the weights, a particular job always comes to the top. So that's an indication that you should seriously consider that job; however, remember that this is just in comparison to the other jobs in the model, so it's possible that adding another prospective job will eliminate the dominance.

2. The other thing to consider is that a particular job want is non-negotiable. No matter what, you have to have that satisfied, then when evaluating each opportunity, you need to assess that want for each prospective job. If it isn't an evaluation 4 (in the case of this model) then you need

to decide if you should even consider taking this job. Note that having too many non-negotiable wants can make finding a job more difficult.

I hope you now see how easy it is to take your Life's Wants and Needs to the job that will satisfy your life.

Chapter Ten

Next Steps

Y ou did it! You made it through a process that can change your life!

Now, let's wrap things up and provide you with additional uses for the products you developed along the way to finding a job that will lead to a satisfying life.

The Job Fit Process:

    1. **Life's Wants and Needs List**

    2. **Career Wants and Needs List**

    3. **Strengths List**

    4. **Weaknesses List**

    5. **Opportunities List**

    6. **Threats List**

    7. **Sweet Spot: Insights into the attributes you want for a specific job**

    8. **Quantitative Decision Tool (QDT): Compare job opportunities**

In addition, the Job Fit Process and these products are reusable as your situation changes. Keep your notes and lists!

The Job Fit Process flowed along the Strategy, Operations, and Tactics path.

Finding a job that fits your life is imperative. Now, the Job Fit Process and your input have put you on a path to finding that job that fits your life!

Your Next Steps: Strengthen your professionalism, communication, and job skills.

RESOURCES

DENNISGUZIK.COM/RESOURCES

Free bonus resources available:
Comprehensive guides, checklists, and
useful spreadsheets to make the job hunt
easier.

BE THE ULTIMATE PODCAST

The Be The Ultimate with Dennis Guzik
podcast is the perfect show for anyone who
wants to achieve professional success.
Available on all major podcast platforms.

CAREERONESTOP.ORG

This site is a great resource and also offers
targeted resources for workers age 55 and
older, veterans, people with a criminal
conviction, and workers with disabilities.

MYSKILLSMYFUTURE.ORG/

Career Changers: Visit CareerOneStop's
mySkills myFuture website to learn how to
put your skills to work in a new career.

If you found this book helpful,
please leave a review on
Amazon.

Thank you!

Dennis Guzik

About the Author: Dennis Guzik

Dennis is unique in the career coaching business. He has the education and experiences few have, to include an extensive background as a Marine Corps officer for over 20 years, almost 20 years in a defense consulting corporation, and a Master of Science degree in quantitative analysis used to aid decision making.

Dennis was raised in northern New Jersey. He attended The Ohio State University on a Naval Reserve Officer Training Corps scholarship and graduated from there with a Bachelor of Science degree in Ceramic Engineering. Dennis was subsequently commissioned as a second lieutenant in the United States Marine Corps. During his Marine Corps career, he served in leadership positions in artillery, infantry, communications, operational planning, distance learning course development, and financial planning.

While in the Marines, Dennis was offered the opportunity to attend the US Naval Postgraduate School, where he graduated with a MS in Operations Research.

Upon leaving the Marine Corps Dennis began work at a large defense consulting firm in the Washington DC area. Dennis rose from senior analyst to project leader, program manager, and eventually Vice President where he led a business unit that provided a quantitative analysis in support of major Marine Corps decisions. During his corporate career, Dennis had the opportunity to review thousands of resumes, conduct hundreds of interviews, and hire and mentor many people.

Dennis left his corporate career to care for his wife whose physical health had many challenges. While home, he continued to mentor others and soon formed Dennis Guzik LLC to continue doing what he had a passion for doing throughout both of his past careers: helping others have a personally and professionally satisfying and successful life.

Dennis's unique career and practical experiences as a leader of Marines, corporate officer, and quantitative analyst led to the development of this book that he guarantees will help you find a job that fits your life!

Made in United States
Troutdale, OR
11/27/2023

14980107R00087